african small publishers' catalogue

2016

Edited and compiled by
Colleen Higgs and Aimee Carelse

African Small Publishers' Catalogue 2016

First published by Modjaji Books 2016
PO Box 121, Rondebosch, 7701, Cape Town, South Africa

www.modjajibooks.co.za
info@modjajibooks.co.za

Editors: Colleen Higgs and Aimee Carelse
Cover image: Toni Olivier
Production: Fire and Lion

ISBN: 978-1-928215-31-8

Contents

Introduction

This is the third edition of the *African Small Publishers' Catalogue*. Once again we have many more publishers and some of the publishers we featured last time have either left the scene, or their circumstances have changed such that they don't want to be in the catalogue. The catalogue is a showcase of the variety and extent of independent and small publishing in Africa. It is still weighted with many more South African publishers, but each time we have brought out a new edition, there are more listings from a wider spread of African publishers. The catalogue aims to uncover and highlight the work and existence of small publishers in Africa. I hope that librarians, booksellers, books' page editors, educators, readers, writers and bigger publishers will be enriched by having access to these publishers and that the publishers themselves will find new customers, access to funds and technologies that will enable them to thrive. It is thrilling to see all the writers and publishers who are toiling away, doing extraordinary creative cultural work.

The editors

Colleen Higgs is a publisher who also writes poetry and short fiction. She has had two poetry collections published: *Halfborn Woman* (2004), *Lava Lamp Poems* (2011) and a collection of short stories: *Looking for Trouble* (2012). She started Modjaji Books in 2007, it has since become an internationally recognized feminist press. Many Modjaji titles have won awards or been short listed. Modjaji Books is a member of the International Alliance of Independent Publishers. Higgs is a publishing activist, and this catalogue is one of the ways she contributes to book development and raising the profile of independent publishing in Africa. She lives in Cape Town with her partner, daughter, three dogs and a cat.

Aimee Carelse is currently completing her Masters degree in Media Theory and Practice in the Centre for Film and Media Studies at the University of Cape Town. Her current research analyses women's engagement with African feminist media blogs, and how this platform blurs the public/private dichotomy, forcing us to reconceptualise notions of women's citizenship in Africa. Aimee works for the Writing Centre in the Centre for Higher Education Development at UCT where she helps first year to PhD students hone and strengthen their academic writing skills. She tutors in both the Centre for Film and Media Studies and the African Gender Institute at UCT. She is also a research fellow of the AW Mellon Foundation in New York. When she has some downtime, Aimee enjoys reading a good psychological or suspense thriller. She is currently reading *The Three* by South African author Sarah Lotz. Next on her list is Modjaji's own *Witch Girl* by Tanvi Bush.

Listings

Aerial Publishing

Address   c/o The Institute for the Study of English in Africa
               Rhodes University, PO Box 6082, Grahamstown, 6140
Email   aerial.publishing.grahamstown@gmail.com
Phone   + 27 046 622 5081

Aerial Publishing is a Grahamstown-based community publisher, publishing mainly previously unpublished Eastern Cape poets. It emerged from the popular four month creative writing course which has been running at the Rhodes Institute for the Study of English in Africa (ISEA) since 1998, when writers associated with the course decided to publish individual collections. As new writers are published, they are invited to become part of the collective which selects, edits and publishes the next books. All money made from sales goes towards the publishing of future titles. Aerial Publishing's first two poetry collections were published in 2004 and 12 titles later we're still going strong.

African Sun Press

Address	PO Box 16415 Vlaeberg 8018 Cape Town
Email address	afpress@iafrica.com
Telephone	+ 27 21 461 1601
Fax	+27 21 461 1601
Website	www.afsun.co.za
Contact	Patricia Schonstein
Associates	Left Field Poetry (London) and the McGregor Poetry Festival

African Sun Press
www.afsun.co.za

We are South Africa's leading poetry anthologists, publishing the *Africa! Anthologies*; the *McGregor Poetry Festival Anthologies*; and *Stanzas* – a quarterly for new poems. We administer the rights of Patricia Schonstein and Don Pinnock and curate the Pinnock Photographic Archive.

Patricia Schonstein is a novelist and poet. Her work is endorsed by Nobel Laureates JM Coetzee and Archbishop Tutu.

Don Pinnock is a former editor of *Getaway*; author of natural history and travel; renowned criminologist; expert on youth-at-risk.

Douglas Reid Skinner is a former editor of *New Contrast* (1988–1992). His poetry is published in five volumes and two books of translations.

AmaBooks

Address	PO Box AC 1066, Ascot, Bulawayo, Zimbabwe
Email	amabooksbyo@gmail.com
Phone	+ 26 3 9 246602
Website	www.amabooksbyo.com
Contact	Jane Morris

amaBooks is a small, independent publisher based in Zimbabwe's second city Bulawayo. We publish novels, short stories, poetry, with a few local history and culture titles. Our main focus is Zimbabwean literary fiction in English, work that reflects contemporary life in the country. Since our inception we have been able to give a platform to many emerging writers, as well as those who are more established. Over 200 writers have now been published by amaBooks. Several of our titles have acheived recognition both nationally and internationally, including those by Tendai Huchu, Bryony Rheam, Togara Muzanenhamo, John Eppel, Christopher Mlalazi and Pathisa Nyathi.

Amalion Publishing

Address	133 Cité Assembleé Ouakam BP 5637, Dakar-Fann, Dakar
Email	publish@amalion.net
Phone	+ 221 33 860 1904
Website	www.amalion.net
Facebook	facebook.com/AmalionPublishing
Twitter	@Amalion
Contact	Sulaiman Adebowale

Amalion Publishing is an independent scholarly publisher with the mission to disseminate innovative knowledge on Africa and to strengthen the understanding of Africa and its people. Amalion provides a platform for authors to express new, alternative and daring perspectives and views on people, places, events, and issues shaping our world. Amalion Publishing produces monographs, textbooks, journals and literary writing – primarily in English and French – for scholars, students, and general readers with an interest in African Studies, the Humanities, and the Social Sciences. Amalion titles are distributed in France and Benelux countries by l'Oiseau Indigo and Bookwitty (www.loiseauindigo.fr), in North America by International Specialized Book Services (www.isbs.com) and in the United Kingdom by Central Books (www.centralbooks.com).

Awesome SA

Address	29 Danville Ave Durban North, South Africa
Post	PO Box 121, Glenashley, 4022
Email	info@awesomesa.co.za
Phone	+ 27 82 786 8450
Website	www.awesomeSApublishers.com
Contact	Derryn Campbell

Awesome SA Publishers are independent publishers who create positive, non-fiction books which are interesting and engaging. First published in 2010 and again in 2015, the best-selling volumes of *Awesome South Africa* make the perfect gift for all ages. The colourful graphic design and photography within the books depict the heart and the soul of the country and are filled with fun, facts and humour and guaranteed to astonish and astound both South Africans and foreigners. The books created by Awesome SA Publishers invite the reader to positively influence the future. Visit our website to view the full range of books.

Awesome SA Publishers

Ayanda Books

SOUTH AFRICA

Address	45 Balsam Street, Zakariyya Park, 1829, South Africa
Post	P O Box 21758, Zakariyya Park, 1821 South Africa
Email	mbls.publishing@gmail.com
Phone	+27 11 859 2471
Website	www.mbls.co.za

Ayanda Books publishes the popular AYANDA titles that simply aim to make children aware of social and political issues that affect them and society as a whole. Age group: 9–13 years. An imprint of MBLS Communications (Pty) Ltd.

Ayebia Clarke Publishing Limited

Address	7 Syringa Walk, Banbury, Oxfordshire, OX16 1FR, UK
Email	ayebia@ayebia.co.uk
Phone	+ 44 1295 709228
Website	www.ayebia.co.uk
Contact	Nana Ayebia Clarke MBE, Managing Director

Ayebia Clarke Publishing Limited is an award-winning independent publisher specializing in quality African and Caribbean literature based in Oxfordshire, UK. Ghanaian-born Publisher Becky Nana Ayebia Clarke was Submissions Editor at the highly regarded African and Caribbean Writers Series at Heinemann Educational Books at Oxford for 12 years where she was part of a team in the International Department that published and promoted prominent and award-winning writers including Wole Soyinka, Ama Ata Aidoo, Chinua Achebe, Ngugi wa Thiong'o, Nadine Gordimer, *et al.* She founded Ayebia with her British husband David in 2003 as a way of looking to new directions in African publishing after Heinemann announced the demise of active publishing in the AWS in 2002. Ayebia's mission is to publish books that will open new spaces and bring fresh insights into African and Caribbean culture and literature internationally. Ayebia's books are currently used for courses on African Studies on Literature, History, Culture, Gender and Postcolonial courses internationally. Becky Nana Ayebia Clarke was awarded an Honorary MBE in 2011 by Her Majesty Queen Elizabeth II for 'services to the UK publishing industry.'

Aztar Press

Address	P.O. Box 768, Morningside, 2057, Gauteng, South Africa
Email	aztarpress@gmail.com
Website	www.aztarpress.com
Facebook	facebook.com/AztarPress
Twitter	@AztarPress
Contact	Judy Croome

In the time-honoured spirit of independent publishing, Aztar Press is committed to publishing outstanding fiction and poetry written outside the norms of the popular establishment. The high-quality print and electronic books released by us will share a common vision of fiction that both entertains the reader and explores the authentic human experience.

Basler Afrika Bibliographien Publishing House

Address	Basler Afrika Bibliographien Publishing House BAB
	Klosterberg 21
	PO Box 2037
	CH-4001 Basel
	Switzerland
Email	publishing@baslerafrika.ch
Phone	+ 41 61 228 93 33
Website	http://baslerafrika.ch

The BAB Publishing House has been publishing scholarly works on Southern Africa, especially Namibia, since 1971. Its thematic emphases are oriented towards the humanities and social sciences. The BAB Publishing House seeks to promote cultural exchange and engagement regarding important contemporary historical issues and, in particular, to provide African scholars with a platform. Our (cultural-) historical, political and anthropological publications are aimed at international academic audiences as well as engaged readers broadly interested in Africa.

Big Bug Books

Address	6 Schroder Street, Stellenbosch
Email	paula@bb-books.co.za
Phone	+ 27 21 8828352 or + 27 828823923
Website	www.bb-books.co.za
Twitter	@BigBugBookscc
Contact	Paula Raubenheimer

Big Bug Books is a graded educational reading and life-skills series for children, ages 5–12 years, featuring the characters KIERIE & KRIEKIE®. The following languages are supported: Afrikaans, Chichewa, English, Hausa, Igbo, isiXhosa, isiZulu, Kinyarwanda, Kiswahili, Luganda, Luo, Shona and Yoruba. Paula Raubenheimer, an occupational therapist wrote and illustrated the readers and Dr. Hannie Menkveld, a foundation/elementary phase educator wrote the teacher manuals. The readers and teacher manuals have free worksheets. All material is available on tablet and mobile phone. We are committed to eradicating illiteracy.

SINDIWE MAGONA
Books 'n Bricks
at Manyano School

Sindiwe Magona in partnership with Dr Al Witten

dp davidphilip

BK Publishing (Pty) Ltd

Address	1239 Francis Baard Street, Hatfield, Pretoria, 0083, South Africa
Post	P.O. Box 6314, Pretoria, 0001, South Africa
Email	mail@bkpublishing.co.za
Phone	+ 27 12 342 5347
Website	www.bkpublishing.co.za
	www.supernovamagazine.co.za
	www.preflightbooks.co.za
Contact	Benoit Knox (Director/Publisher)

BK Publishing is a vibrant publishing house in the heart of Pretoria. Our entrepreneurial spirit has manifested itself in the great variety of projects, imprints and services we provide. To fulfil our vision of fostering a book loving and book buying culture, we have created *Supernova*, the magazine for curious kids. With *Supernova* and other products for reluctant readers, we aim to make children aware of issues which affect them, their community and their environment. We give them the tools and inspiration to become active and responsible world citizens. With over 10 years of experience and a collection of wonderful original publications, our indie imprint, Preflight Books, helps aspiring authors and self-publishers bring their manuscripts to life. Black & Bright, our design division, offers all the design and communication solutions you need to take your business to the next level.

Black Letter Media

SOUTH AFRICA

Address	The Main Change (Open), 4th Floor, 20 Kruger Street
	Maboneng, Johannesburg
Post	P.O. Box 94004, Yeoville, 2198
Email	info@blackletterm.com
Phone	+ 27 84 849 8670
Website	www.blackletterm.com
Facebook	facebook.com/BlackLetterMedia
Contact	Duduzile Mabaso

Black Letter Media is a publishing and booksellng company which focuses on creating platforms online or in print for new African storytellers to publish their vision of Africa and for African readers to discover, new,  independent African literature. We do this through platforms such as poetrypotion.com, and print books including the Poetry Potion quarterly, short story collections and novels. Our bookselling platform is the online market for independently produced African literature Book Lover's Market – bookloversmarket.com. Our writers and publishers are primarily based in South African but include Nigeria, Uganda, Cameroon, Kenya, Zimbabwe, Uganda, Cameroon and Botswana.

Blue Weaver

SOUTH AFRICA

Address	PO Box 30370, Tokai, Cape Town, 7966, South Africa
Email	admin@blueweaver.co.za
Phone	+ 27 21 701 4477
Website	www.blueweaver.co.za
Facebook	www.facebook.com/blueweavertrade
Twitter	@blueweavertrade
Contact	Louise Nichols or Natasha Store

Blue Weaver is a fully independent book marketing, sales and distribution company based in Cape Town, South Africa. The company represents several of the most respected specialist General, Trade, Academic and Scholarly Publishers in the country. Further, Blue Weaver represents and distributes for a growing number of similar, like-minded International Publishers.

Bookcraft Ltd

Address	23 Adebajo Street, Kongi Layout, Ibadan, Nigeria
Post	GPO Box 16729, Dugbe, Ibadan, Oyo State, Nigeria
Email	info@bookcraftafrica.com
Phone	+ 234 8033447889; +234 8073199967; +234 8037220773
Website	www.bookcraftafrica.com
Facebook	facebook.com/BookcraftAfrica
Twitter	@bookcraftafrica
Contact	Dapo Olugbade

Bookcraft Ltd is a publishing company. We have published a large number of titles in a wide variety of subjects: art, biography, history, literature, politics, and current affairs. We publish for a growing market of discerning, sophisticated and well educated bibliophiles. Our books' uniquely packaged, reader friendly design makes them instantly recognizable.

Book Dash

Email   team@bookdash.org
Phone   + 27 82 099 4414
Website   www.bookdash.org
Contact   Julia Norrish

At Book Dash, we believe every child should own a hundred books by the age of five. This means creating and distributing large numbers of new, African storybooks in local languages.

To make this possible, we gather creative professionals to create high-quality children's books that anyone can freely download, print, translate and distribute. We then work with funders and literacy and ECD organisations to print and give away books in large volumes. Funders and partner organisations are encouraged to visit our website and get in contact with us.

Bookstorm (Pty) Ltd

Address   304 Castle Hill Drive, Blackheath, 2195
Johannesburg, South Africa

Post   PO Box 4532, Northcliff, Johannesburg, 2115, South Africa

Email   info@bookstorm.co.za

Phone   + 27 11 478 6020

Website   www.bookstorm.co.za

Facebook   facebook.com/Bookstorm

Bookstorm is a boutique book publishing company offering focused experience and innovation in the creation of books for the South African market. Bookstorm was founded in 2010 by Louise Grantham and Basil van Rooyen, both experienced trade publishers with a long history of publishing for the South African general reading market. We publish in a variety of genres including business, entrepreneurship, economics, investment, current affairs, cookery, health, sports and travel. Our books are written by a range of select South African authors who represent a diversity of skills and opinions. Bookstorm also offers agency distribution, corporate publishing services and self-publishing services under its Rainbird imprint.

Breeze Publishing cc

SOUTH AFRICA

Address   15 Lavery Crescent, Overport, 4091, Durban, South Africa
Email   breezepublishing@gmail.com
Phone   + 27 791079930
Facebook   facebook.com/breezepublishingcc
Contact   Naseema Mall

Breeze Publishing is set on publishing quality books of a variety of themes and categories, both in fiction and non-fiction; for the adult, teen and children's markets. Breeze Publishing  is constantly being approached by both local and foreign authors, and continues to carefully select manuscripts of quality. The company has great aspirations to become a dominant player in a very versatile but restricted market and hopes to affiliate itself with both budding as well as established authors, so that it can grow with them to greater heights.

Burnet Media

Address   PO Box 53557, Kenilworth, 7745, Cape Town, South Africa
Email   info@burnetmedia.co.za
Phone   + 27 21 404 1450
Website   www.burnetmedia.co.za
Facebook   facebook.com/TwoDogsMercury
Contact   Tim Richman

Burnet Media is an independent publisher based in Cape Town. We produce books for two main imprints – Two Dogs and Mercury, established in 2006 and 2011 respectively – as well as various customised publishing projects. We also offer publishing consulting and production services. Our aim is to build close and interactive relationships with our authors and clients and, in doing so, create interesting and innovative South African titles. Jacana Media markets our titles into the trade. On The Dot is our distributor.

Cassava Republic Press

Address	62B, Arts and Crafts Village, Opposite Sheraton Hotel
	Abuja, Nigeria
Email	editor@cassavarepublic.biz
Phone	+ 234 09 780 3159
Website	www.cassavarepublic.biz
Facebook	facebook.com/CassavaRepublic
Twitter	@CassavaRepublic
Contact	Bibi Bakare-Yusuf

We publish literary fiction, non-fiction, crime fiction, children's and young adult fiction and non-fiction. We have just launched a new romance series, Ankara Press.

Chimurenga

Address	Room 303, Pan African Market, 76 Long Street, Cape Town, South Africa
Post	Chimurenga Magazine, PO Box 15117, Vlaeberg, 8018, Cape Town, South Africa
Email	chimurenga@panafrican.co.za
	info@chimurenga.co.za
Phone	+ 27 21 422 4168
Website	www.chimurenga.co.za
Facebook	facebook.com/Chimurenga
Twitter	@Chimurenga_SA

Chimurenga is a journal of writing, art, culture and politics published out of Cape Town. Since its first issue (2002), *Chimurenga* has received excellent reviews for its originality, the quality of its content and its willingness to tackle subjects other publications might consider too difficult or controversial to address. Moreover, several contributors have won international awards for their work published in *Chimurenga*: Binyavanga Wainaina, Yvonne Adhiambo Owuor, Ishtiyaq Shukri, Chimamanda Ngozi Adichie and Seffi Atta to name a few.

Clockwork Books

SOUTH AFRICA

Address	34 Scully Street, Roosevelt Park, Gauteng, 2195
Post	PO Box 44224, Linden, 2104
Email	info@worktheclock.co.za
Phone	+ 27 82 853 8154
Website	www.ClockworkBooks.co.za
Facebook	facebook.com/ClockworkBooksZA
Contact	Sarah McGregor

Passionate about exceptional South African fiction and non-fiction, Clockwork Books is a virtual publishing hub servicing authors and readers alike. Focussing on partnering with authors to produce high quality print books and ebooks, we aim to make the most of the digital space, empower authors to be in control of their work and improve the connection between creators and their communities. We also provide publishing services to self-publishers.

Cover2Cover Books

Address	85 Main Road, Muizenberg, Cape Town, 7945
Email	info@cover2cover.co.za
Phone	+ 27 21 709 0128
Website	cover2cover.co.za
Facebook	facebook.com/cover2cover1
Twitter	@Cover2CoverB

Cover2Cover Books aims to get young South Africans reading by publishing exciting stories that relate to their lives. Our flagship series, Harmony High is set in a fictional township high school, and follows the lives, loves and challenges of a group of young people.

cover2cover books

Cover2Cover continues to grow, and is currently launching two new series – Soccer Season, set in a teen soccer club, and Shadow Chasers, a fantasy series aimed at readers of 8–12 year olds. We also publish FunDza's exciting short story anthologies as well as YA trade fiction. Our non-fiction imprint, Face2Face, showcases South African memoirs, continuing in our tradition of publishing uniquely South African stories.

David Philip Publishers, trading as New Africa Books

Address	1st Floor, 6 Spin Street, Cape Town, 8001, South Africa
Post	PostNet Suite 144, Private Bag X9190
	Cape Town, 8000, South Africa
Email	info@newafricabooks.co.za
Phone	+ 27 21 467 5860
Contact	Dusanka Stojakovic

We publish African books, by African authors and illustrators. The new struggle in South Africa is the low literacy rates, and we publish books for children and young adults that reflect our various cultures. We also have a treasure trove of great books for adults, written by a number of well-known authors, including Richard Rive and Sindiwe Magona.

richard rive
ADVANCE, RETREAT

richard rive
WRITING BLACK

richard rive
'BUCKINGHAM PALACE', DISTRICT SIX

richard rive
EMERGENCY

richard rive
EMERGENCY CONTINUED

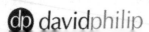

dp davidphilip

Deep South

Address   PO Box 6082 Market Square Grahamstown 6141
Email   r.berold@gmail.com
Phone   + 27 46 622 5081
Contact   Robert Berold

Deep South specialises in South African writing, mostly poetry. The press is run by Robert Berold. Local and international distribution is handled by University of KwaZulu-Natal Press. 21 titles have been published since 2000 including books by Seitlhamo Motsapi, Ari Sitas, Angifi Dladla, Joan Metelerkamp, Khulile Nxumalo, Mzwandile Matiwana, Robert Berold, Kobus Moolman, Mxolisi Nyewa, Vonani Bila and Lesego Rampolokeng.

Éditions Graines de Pensées

Address	30, Boulevard du 13 Janvier, Nyékonakpoè – Lomé 07 B.P. 7097
Email	grainesdepensees@yahoo.com
Phone	+ 228 90 32 33 20
	+ 228 22 22 32 43
Website	www.afrilivres.net
Facebook	facebook.com/editions.grainesdepensees
Twitter	@gpensees
Contact	Mrs Yasmin Issaka-Coubageat

At Graines de Pensées we want to participate in African cultural expression, to contribute, with our books, to the development of a democratic and pluralist society, with the ability to criticize and respond to social issues. As publishers we are keen to give to this new African generation books which are accessible, that they can relate to, and that have a very high editorial quality. Furthermore, for a better distribution of our books, we participate in co-publishing projects, with partners in countries in both the South and the North. We also create business relationships with various institutions and companies for the better promotion of books in French, English and in African languages.

Femrite – Uganda Women Writers Association

Address	Kira Road Plot 147, 705, Kampala, Uganda
Email	info@femriteug.org
Phone	+ 256 414 543 943
Website	www.femriteug.org
Facebook	
facebook.com/Uganda-Women-Writers-Association-FEMRITE-159169540775181	
Twitter	@ugwomenwriters
Contact	Executive Director Ms Hilda Twongyeirwe

FEMRITE publishes fiction and creative non-fiction which is mainly written by women. From establishment, the organization was aimed at training, promoting and publishing women writers. This still has a big bearing on what is published because women's situations which led to the establishing of the organization have not changed substantially. However, FEMRITE has included male writers in its programmes because both male and female writers operate under the same infrastructure and some issues such as limited publishing opportunities affect them in the same way.

FIRE AND LION

High-quality book and ebook production

Fire and Lion helps publishers manage their
book-making, lowering their costs and freeing their
time to focus on authors and special projects.

Our team combines world-class design and
digital expertise, built on a deep understanding
of book publishing.

team@fireandlion.com | www.fireandlion.com

Fourthwall Books

Address	52 Dundalk Avenue
	Unit No. 5
	Parkview, 2193
	Johannesburg
Email	info@fourthwallbooks.com
Phone	+ 27 82 858 0247
Website	www.fourthwallbooks.com
Facebook	www.facebook.com/FourthwallBooks
Contact	Bronwyn Law-Viljoen

Fourthwall Books was established in
Johannesburg in 2010 by designer Oliver
Barstow and editor Bronwyn Law-Viljoen.
Back then we had one simple goal in mind: to
publish art and artists' books, photography books and books on
architecture and the city (Johannesburg in particular) that we ourselves
would like to own; books that were out of the ordinary—provocative,
experimental, well designed, interesting to read, gratifying to hold and
look at. We're still pursuing that goal, though perhaps with a little more
clarity than before and also having learned a few important things about
books along the way.

FW

Geko Publishing

Address	40 Morsim Road, Hyde Park, Joburg
Email	write@gekopublishing.co.za
Phone	+ 27 83 991 6647
Website	http://gekopublishing.co.za
Facebook	facebook.com/GekoPublishingSA
Twitter	@GekoPublishing
Contact	Phehello Mofokeng

We publish what makes us happy – from poetry, music biographies, fiction (novels, short stories etc), fantasy and most importantly folklore/folktales in English and in African languages. Go to our website to download or read submission guidelines before submitting anything.

geko publishing
freedom to write.

Green is Not a Colour / The Lightning Lab

Address	5 Cherry Street, Newlands, Cape Town
Email	info@thelightninglab.org
Website	www.greenisnotacolour.org
Facebook	facebook.com/greenisnotacolour
Twitter	@EnvironmentE
Contact	Devan Valenti

The Lightning Lab is a young, innovative think tank dedicated to the widespread advancement of environmental education, and the adoption of sustainable designs, technologies and processes on both a local and global scale. We achieve this through fresh, creative and insightful forms of communication intended to inspire and motivate others to action. The Lightning Lab has embarked on this vision with the publication of its first book titled *Green Is Not A Colour: Environmental issues Every Generation Needs To Know*.

Groenheide Boeke

SOUTH AFRICA

Address	PO Box 508, Hartenbos 6520, South Africa
Email	admin@groenheide.co.za
Website	www.groenheide.co.za

Uitgewers van Die Poniehoewe-Klub en ander lekkerlees boeke vir jonk en oud.

Happy Readers Zimbabwe

Address	23 Guys Cliff, Harare, Zimbabwe
Post	P.O. Box BW 773, Borrowdale, Harare, Zimbabwe
Email	happybooks.emma@gmail.com
	happybooks.conor@gmail.com
Phone	+ 263 77 238 6163
	+ 263 (04) 88 37 35
Website	www.happy-readers.com
Facebook	facebook.com/happyreaderszimbabwe
Twitter	@HappyReadersZim
Contact	Emma O'Beirne

Happy Readers are all you need to read! A specifically structured reading program for children with ESOL – books, teacher training, class resources and M & E implementation in conjunction with donor partners. Primarily aimed at Grades 1 & 2, but frequently used throughout schools as remedial readers. Our books are fun, happy, brightly coloured and use animals as characters in familiar rural and urban settings. Happy Readers promote positive African values as well as sensitising children and teachers to gender specific issues, best cultural practices and better world themes. Ministry of Education approved for use in schools in Zimbabwe and Zambia.

OVER **2000** TITLES IN OUR CATALOGUE

147 INDEPENDENT & AUTONOMOUS AFRICAN PUBLISHERS FROM **25** COUNTRIES

OVER **20000** BOOKS SOLD ANNUALLY

OVER **$3M** REMITTED TO AFRICAN PUBLISHERS

39 SUBJECT DISCIPLINES

200 NEW TITLES EACH YEAR

AFRICAN BOOKS COLLECTIVE

AFRICAN BOOKS COLLECTIVE (ABC), founded, owned and governed by African publishers, seeks to strengthen African publishing through collective action and to increase the visibility and accessibility of the wealth of African scholarship and culture.

***

ABC is a non-profit Oxford-based, worldwide marketing and distribution outlet for 2,500 print titles from Africa, of which 800 are also ebooks - scholarly, literature and children's books.

***

ABC seeks to be the primary distribution choice for independent African publishers; to provide the most comprehensive selection of relevant material to customers worldwide in the form they require; to achieve ABC's cultural aims whilst operating in a wholly commercial space; and to grow the market for African books worldwide.

***

Titles stocked are from many of the leading publishers in Africa: scholarly, literary, art books, children's books, and books in African languages and in translation. They are available in print, and many also as ebooks, in European and some African languages.

REPRESENTING

10 PAN AFRICAN RESEARCH INSTITUTES

SINCE 1989

SINGLE

SOURCE

AWARD WINNING TITLES

WORLDWIDE SHIPPING

PO BOX 721
OXFORD OX1 9EN
OF SUPPLY UNITED KINGDOM

TEL/FAX +44 (0) 1869 349110

SHOP ONLINE

WWW.AFRICANBOOKSCOLLECTIVE.COM

BEST OF AFRICAN PUBLISHING. SINGLE SOURCE OF SUPPLY.

Junkets Publisher

SOUTH AFRICA

Address	11 Winchester Road, Observatory
Email	info.junkets@iafrica.com
Phone	+ 27 76 169 2789
Website	www.junkets.co.za
Facebook	facebook.com/groups/Junkets
	facebook.com/Junketspublisher
	facebook.com/Junkets10Series
Contact	Andi Mgibantaka and Robin Malan

Junkets Publisher is a small not-for-profit independent publisher that specialises in high-quality low-cost new South African playscripts. We publish the Playscript Series of individual plays, the Collected Series of anthologies of plays, and now the Junkets10Series of ten new plays celebrating our tenth birthday. The BaxterJunkets series publishes the winning play of each year's Zabalaza Theatre Festival. GayJunkets publishes queer-interest books in various genres. The first book we published in 2005 was 'Rebel Angel', a novel based on the life of John Keats. 'Junkets' is Leigh Hunt's nickname for him: Jun-Kets. Our logo is Keats's autograph.

Kachifo Limited

Address	253 Herbert Macaulay Way, Yaba, Lagos, Nigeria
Email	info@kachifo.com
Phone	+ 23 48077364217
Website	www.kachifo.com; farafinabooks.wordpress.com
Facebook	facebook.com/Farafina-Kachifo-154905034600561
Twitter	@farafinabooks

Kachifo Limited, an independent Nigerian publishing house, began operations in 2004  driven by the words of its motto and mission statement, Telling our own Stories. Its imprint, Farafina, has published works of fiction, memoirs, and poetry with an African audience in mind. It continues to receive unsolicited submissions at submissions@kachifo.com.

Kalahari Publishers and Booksellers

Address	116 ERF Mphaphuli, Makwarela Road, Next to Exel Sibasa, 0970
Email	info@kpb.co.za
Phone	+ 27 15 963 1529
Website	www.kpb.co.za
Contact	Themba Patrick Magaisa (Xitsonga Publisher)

Kwani Trust

KENYA

Address	PO Box 2895-00100, Nairobi, Kenya
Email	sales@kwani.org
Phone	+ 254 70 483 2379; +254 20 444 1801
Website	www.kwani.org
Facebook	facebook.com/kwanitrust
Twitter	@kwanitrust

Kwani Trust is a regional literary hub and a community of writers that is committed to the growth of the region's creative industry through publishing and distributing contemporary African literature, offering training opportunities, producing literary events and establishing global literary networks.

Learn to Read – Read to Learn

Address	45 Balsam Street, Zakariyya Park, 1829, South Africa
Post	P O Box 21758, Zakariyya Park, 1821 South Africa
Email	mbls.publishing@gmail.com
Phone	+ 27 11 859 2471
Website	www.mbls.co.za
Contact	Manichand Beharilal

Publishes books with mostly South African terminology to help pre-schoolers and first graders increase vocabulary. Age group: 5 – 6 years. These books are published for the South African Literacy Foundation. An imprint of MBLS Communications (Pty) Ltd.

Les Classiques Africains

Address   25 Club Road, Vacoas, Mauritius
Email   info@lesclassiquesafricains.com
Phone   + 230 601 14 84
Website   www.lesclassiquesafricains.com
Facebook   facebook.com/les.classiques.africains

Originally a French publishing house, Les Classiques Africains was bought in 2006 by a Mauritian company. Renowned all over Frenchspeaking African countries for more than 50 years, our catalogue now offers more than 200 titles in various fields: school textbooks, practical guides, religious books and children's books. Based in Mauritius, our team is dedicated to publishing affordable books of excellent quality.

Liquid Type Publishing Services

Address	1891 Hearn Road, Henley on Klip, Midvaal, South Africa, 1961
Post	P.O. Box 448, Henley on Klip, 1962
Email	wesley@liquidtype.co.za
Phone	+ 27 726495274
Website	www.liquidtype.co.za
Contact	Wesley Thompson
Twitter	@liquidType

Liquid Type Publishing Services is a specialised book-publishing services company that offers exceptional editing, ebook design, project management, proofreading and self-publishing services to authors, companies and publishers. Liquid Type's work is characterised by fine attention to detail, sound publishing advice and the highest book-production standards. Please contact me to discuss all things bookish.

WHAT WE DO

Blue Weaver has been assisting and working with Small Publishers and Self Published Authors since 2001.

The role that **Blue Weaver** plays is to assist in bridging the main divide between Self-Publishing and having your book published with a traditional Publisher. With a traditional publisher, book store distribution is one of the main arguments for publishing with a traditional press. In this regard, **Blue Weaver** offers the following:

- Providing our Clients with a direct marketing, sales and distribution infrastructure in South Africa and key International markets, allowing them to compete effectively in the market place.

- A dedicated Sales Force calling on Bookshop Chains and Independent Bookshops throughout South Africa who have developed long-term relationships with important booksellers over the years.

- A focus on niche markets for individual genres outside of the traditional book retail markets.

- Interacting, selling and promoting to Interest Groups through our various Social Media platforms.

- We work closely with and can refer you to experts for help with design, editing, e-book conversion, printing and other tasks in order to publish your book.

While we tend to focus mainly on Non-Fiction we do support works of fiction that are accompanied and supported with good Media and Publicity.

Please see our Website **www.blueweaver.co.za** to find

Martial Publishing

Address	P O Box 11579, Klein Windhoek, Windhoek
Email	bryony@martialpublishing.com
Phone	+ 264 61 400 553
Website	www.martialpublishing.com
Contact	Bryony van Der Merwe

Martial Publishing takes pride in sharing good literature with the world, hence our slogan "Books without Boundaries". We mainly publish novels and enjoy introducing the characters and their stories to our readers. We believe that very diverse groups of people can be united by the written word. Although the company is based in Namibia, our books are distributed to a worldwide audience, and we accept submissions from all over the world. We do not publish poetry or short stories, nor do we publish in languages other than English at this time.

MaThoko's Books

Address	PO Box 31719, Braamfontein, 2017, South Africa
Email	info@gala.co.za
Phone	+ 27 11 717 4239
Website	www.gala.co.za/cultural_heritage/ma_thokos_books.htm
Facebook	facebook.com/MathokosBooks

MaThoko's Books is the publishing imprint of Gay and Lesbian Memory in Action (GALA). Launched in 2011, the imprint aims to be a corrective to the limited publishing support for queer writing in Africa and to act as a springboard for emerging and marginalised voices. It also provides a much-needed publishing outlet for scholarly works on LGBTIQ-related themes. MaThoko's Books was founded on a belief that the sharing of stories can help to challenge homophobia and transphobia. The imprint is committed to publishing high-quality writing that not only helps to educate the public about sexuality and gender identity but that also promotes human rights on the African continent.

MBLS Publishing

Address	45 Balsam Street, Zakariyya Park, 1829, South Africa
Post	P O Box 21758, Zakariyya Park, 1821 South Africa
Email	mbls.publishing@gmail.com
Phone	+ 27 11 859 2471
Website	www.mbls.co.za
Facebook	facebook.com/MBLS-Publishing-318042515064830/info

MBLS Publishing publishes children's book under the imprints THEMBI AND THEMBA BOOKS, AYANDA BOOKS and LEARN TO READ – READ TO LEARN for reading at the library and to educate in the classroom; informing and educating children about institutions and societal issues to contribute to their development as caring and responsible young adults.

Modjaji Books

Address	PO Box 121, Rondebosch, 7701, Cape Town, South Africa
Email	info@modjajibooks.co.za
Phone	+ 21 6965503
Website	www.modjajibooks.co.za
Facebook	facebook.com/Modjajibooks
Twitter	@modjaji_bks
Contact	Colleen Higgs

An independent publishing company based in Cape Town, South Africa. We publish books by southern African women writers. We publish novels, short stories, memoir, biography, poetry, essays, narrative non-fiction and award-winning women writers with brave voices.

The history of publishing in South Africa is enmeshed with the culture of resistance that flourished under apartheid. 'Struggle' literature may have emerged from the 'underground', but women's voices – particularly black women's voices – are still marginalised. Modjaji Books addresses this inequality by publishing books that are true to the spirit of Modjaji the rain queen: a powerful female force for good, growth, new life, regeneration.

The Skin We Are In

Introducing a new book about the evolution of human skin colour!

Join Njabulo, Aisha, Tim, Chris and Roshni as they discover why humans have different skins, and how people's thinking about skin colour has changed throughout history. *The Skin We Are In* is a celebration of the glorious human rainbow, both in South Africa and beyond.

by Sindiwe Magona and Nina G. Jablonski
Illustrated by Lynn Fellman

NF Saliwa Publishing cc

Address	5 Coriander Crescent, Vredenberg, Bellville, 7530
Post	5 Coriander Crescent, Vredenberg, Bellville, 7530
Email	ncebakazi@nfsaliwa.co.za
Phone	+ 27 83 3369639
Website	www.nfsaliwa.co.za
Contact	Faith Saliwa

NF Saliwa Publishing cc publishes children's books mainly in African languages to help African language speakers to enhance their reading and writing abilities. The idea was born out of a cry that there were a few children's books published in African languages. The books are written and illustrated by African languages speakers and are set in an African context. We have books for ages 0–12, both general books and educational books. They are available in all South African-African languages. Some of the stories have been translated into English from various African language stories.

Poetree Publications (Pty) Ltd

Address	217 Textile House, Kerk Street, Johannesburg
Post	217 Textile House, 125 Kerk Street, Johannesburg, 2000
Email	poetflow@live.com
Phone	+ 2773 652 0275
Facebook	www.facebook.com/poetreepub
Twitter	@PoetreeBooks
Contact	Selome Payne (Flow)

Poetree Publications strives to provide affordable and accessible publishing services to writers of all genres, and change the perceptions of self-publishing as a whole. The mission is to make a significant contribution to the amount of new and modern written works within the literature industry, primarily in the African literature scene. Poetree aims to immortalise and preserve the stories and indigenous languages of writers, especially the youth, by offering self-publishing services for poetry, fiction/non-fiction, children's stories, motivational books, short stories and more. Services include publishing in print and e-formats.

Poets Printery

Phone	+ 27 82 202 6155
Email	amitabh@amitabhmitra.com
Website	www.poetsprintery.co.za OR www.poetspritnery.book.co.za
Contact	Amitabh Mitra

Poetry doesn't sell, but we are here to sell poetry in stapled/perfect binding and even as coffee table books. We are into buying poetry, vintage poetry books whose authors have passed away or who wants us to redesign their poetry books and market it for them. We would love to publish them again in a new format. We are also an online poetry publisher and compete annually for the prestigious Pushcart Award. If you are a poet/artist and do not have the means to be published, we would be the only one globally for you.

Porcupine Press

SOUTH AFRICA

Address	No. 2 Anikehof Complex, Martha Road North (off Rabie Road)
	Fontainebleau, Randburg, 2194
Post	PO Box 2756, Pinegowrie, 2123 South Africa
Phone	+ 27 11 791 4561
Website	www.porcupinepress.co.za
Facebook	facebook.com/PorcupinePressPage
Twitter	@Porcupine_PRESS
Contact	Gail Robbins

Independent publishing since 2009. Ask your self-publishers how they make their money. What percentage comes from book production? What percentage comes from book sales? Now ask Porcupine the same question. The answer is: throughout 2015 the split was 50/50. We sell what we produce because: • Quality is our non-negotiable. Quality content – quality design – quality printing • Our distribution works. We deal directly with all major bookshop chains and independents – we offer international services – we know how to work the e-book markets. We also distribute for other small publishers and independent authors.

SA Book Council

Address	Tijger Park 3, 2nd Floor, Room 202
	Willie van Schoor, Bellville, 7530
Post	PO Box 583, Sanlamhof, 7532
Email	admin@sabookcouncil.co.za
Phone	+ 27 21 914 8626
Website	www.sabookcouncil.co.za
Contact	Raynia Gaffoor

The Indigenous Languages Publishing Programme is one of the SABDC's programmes to stimulate growth and development in the sector. It aims to increase indigenous languages publishing and to support the ongoing production of South-African-authored

SOUTH AFRICAN BOOK DEVELOPMENT COUNCIL

books in the local languages. The SABDC bi-annually invites registered publishing companies to submit applications for the publishing of children and youth creative works (including novels, short stories, children's literature, etc.) Each submission should be an original work written in one of 9 local languages. (Excluding Afrikaans and English), This programme also contributes to the transformation imperatives of the SABDC. More information on the programme is available on the website.

SAfAIDS Materials Development and Production Services

Address	17 Beveridge Road, Avondale, Harare, Zimbabwe
Email	katrina@safaids.net
Phone	+ 263 4 336193/4
Website	www.safaids.net
Contact	Katrina Wallace-Karenga
Twitter	@SAfAIDS

We promote: effective and ethical development responses on SRHR, HIV and TB prevention, treatment and care. We provide: complete information and communications packages, as  well as in-house services such as: training and facilitation; editing, content development, translation, design and layout; professional management of the print finish on all products; excellence in targeted information development and production, enabling you to communicate effectively with your target audience through services from:

- Branding;
- Conceptualisation and content development;
- Editing;
- Translation and back translation;
- Design and layout; to
- Final production and printing.

Sedia

Address   BP 231, Al Mohammadia, Alger
Email   sedia@sedia-dz.com
                   nkhiat@sedia-dz.com
Phone   + 231 77 097 3861
Website   www.sedia-dz.com
Facebook   facebook.com/sediaalgiers
Contact   Nacéra Khiat

Sedia – Société d'édition et de Diffusion Internationale Algérienne – is an Algerian publishing house, which specialized in school books at the beginning in 2000, then, in 2006,  it has widened its editorial line to general literature with its first collection Mosaique whose concept was republished in Algeria, Algerian renowned authors published abroad, mainly in France.

By the quality of its books and the reputation of its authors, Sedia wants to participate in the evolution of Algerian books and reading promotion. Today, its catalogue contains over a hundred titles, in Arabic and French, and several collections of literature (novels, essays, interviews, children's books).

Sefsafa Culture & Publishing

Address	4 Soliman Gohar Sq. Dokki, Giza. Egypt
Email	elbaaly@gmail.com
	info@sefsafa.net
Phone	+ 201110787870; + 201275324306
Website	www.sefsafa.net
Facebook	facebook.com/sefsafa
Twitter	@Sefsafapub
Contact	Mohamed El-Baaly

Sefsafa Culture & Publishing is a small group based in Egypt, working under the umbrella of 'Sefsafa Culture & Publishing'. We have had a publishing house since 2009, and have published over 100 titles, one third of them translations. The group has also organized the Cairo Literature Festival since 2015, and the Egypt Comix Week festival since 2014. Sefsafa aims to support the enlightenment and Arab Spring ideals.

Shama Books

Address	PO Box 57, Piazza, in front of Cathedral School
	Addis Ababa, Ethiopia
Email	shama@ethionet.et
	gbagersh@shamaethipia.com
Phone	+251 11 554 5290
Website	www.shamaethiopia.com
Contact	Ghassan Bagersh

Shama Books, fully owned by the Bagersh family, has been involved in the publishing of books since 1999, making it the premier mass market publisher in Ethiopia. Shama boasts a burgeoning publishing house that attracts the finest Ethiopian writers, as well as many established foreign authors. Shama, with a mission of improving literacy at all levels and fostering a reading culture in the country, has published over a hundred titles.

In addition to operating a chain of BookWorld bookshops we also operate newsstands and souvenir shops in the major five star hotels in Addis Ababa.

to

affirm

Afrika.

always.

black
letter
media

poetry | short stories | novels
http://blackletterm.com

Siber Ink

Address	B2A Westlake Square, 1 Westlake Drive, Westlake, 7945
Email	simon@siberink.co.za
Phone	+ 27 82 4127780
Website	www.siberink.co.za
Facebook	facebook.com/SiberInk
Twitter	@SiberInk
Contact	Simon Sephton

We publish accessible and authoritative law and business books aimed at lawyers, students and business people or those who are not lawyers and need to know about law (eg HR people or shop stewards who need to know about labour law). We believe that law made simple should not lose its authority; and that no-one should be denied access to legal texts by obscure language.

Siber **Ink**

Sooo Many Stories

Address	Plot 3003 Bbuye Ntinda
Post	P.O. Box 3057
Email	kaboozi@somanystories.ug
Phone	+ 256 776 250 832
Website	http://somanystories.ug
Facebook	facebook.com/sooomanystories
Contact	Nyana Kakoma

UGANDA

Sooo Many Stories started as a blog with the sole aim of showcasing Ugandan Literature. 18 months later the blog has morphed into a publishing house with it's first publication due in 2016. Sooo Many Stories publishes all genres of fiction and creative non-fiction for adults and young adults. We are passionate about making literature accessible to as many people as possible and helping reluctant readers realise that reading can be fun.

Story Press Africa

Address	43 Burger Street, Pietermaritzburg, 3201, South Africa
Post	P.O. Box 22106, Mayor's Walk, 3208, South Africa
Email	info@storypressafrica.com
Phone	+ 27 33 342 9382
Website	www.storypressafrica.com
Contact	Robert Inglis

Story Press Africa, an imprint of Jive Media Africa (South Africa) and Catalyst Book Press (USA), is a platform for African knowledge from Africa. Through the medium of stories (including graphic novels, young adult and children's literature, and picture books) we aim to place African knowledge—its history, science, folklore and art—in its rightful place among the knowledge of the world. We publish stories by and about Africans and Africa for a global audience – authentic, excellent, challenging and frequently controversial visions of the continent that birthed humankind.

Storymoja Africa Ltd

Address	Njamba House, Shanzu Road off Lower Kabete Road, Nairobi
Post	PO Box 264 – 00606, Sarit Centre, Nairobi
Email	info@storymojaafrica.co.ke
Phone	+ 254 772413323; 020 2089595; 0728 285021; 0733 838161
Website	www.storymojaafrica.co.ke
Facebook	facebook.com/Storymojaafrica
Twitter	@Storymoja
Contact	Monity Odera

Storymoja was formed by writers who are committed to publishing contemporary East African writing of world-class standards. To date, Storymoja has published over seventy children's books. The motto is to get a book in every hand.

Est. 2005

ve team of passic

d graphic designe

proudly South Af

ore about our

magazine.co.za   preflightbo

P.O. Box 6314
Pretoria
South Africa
0001

StoryTime

Email   storytime.publishing@gmail.com
Website   http://storytime-african-publisher.blogspot.com
Contact   Ivor W. Hartmann

StoryTime is a micro African press dedicated to
publishing short fiction by emerging and established
African writers. We publish two serial anthologies:
African Roar and *AfroSF*.

Techmate Publishers Ltd

Address   PO Box 6667, Accra North, Ghana

Email   techmatepublishers@gmail.com

Phone   + 233 24 426 2098

Contact   Heena Karamchandani

Our aim is to publish local authors' work so their works are made available to the general public and at a moderate price. We are also working on developing children's books.

Thembi and Themba Books

Address	45 Balsam Street, Zakariyya Park, 1829, South Africa
Post	P O Box 21758, Zakariyya Park, 1821 South Africa
Email	mbls.publishing@gmail.com
Phone	+ 27 11 859 2471
Website	www.mbls.co.za

Publishes the popular THEMBI AND THEMBA titles to inform and educate children about issues and institutions that they will take responsibility for when they grow up; thus aiding in their development as caring, young and responsible adults. Age group: 9 – 14 years. These titles are written and designed to promote reading at the library and to educate in the classroom. An imprint of MBLS Communications (Pty) Ltd.

uHlanga

Address	4 Royalton, 25 Old Bush Road, La Lucia, 4051, South Africa
Post	4 Royalton, 25 Old Bush Road, La Lucia, South Africa, 4051
Email	editorial@uhlangapress.co.za
Phone	+ 27 83 645 1412
Website	www.uhlangapress.co.za
Facebook	facebook.com/uhlanga
Twitter	@uHlangaPress
Contact	Nick Mulgrew

Founded in 2014, uHlanga is South Africa's progressive poetry press, publishing debut collections from South Africa's most promising poets under the uHlanga New Poets imprint, as well as more experimental poetry projects under their eponymous flagship imprint.

Weaver Press

Address	38 Broadlands Road, Emerald Hill, Harare, Zimbabwe
Post	P.O. Box A1922, Avondale, Harare, Zimbabwe
Email	weaveradmin@mango.zw
Phone	+ 263 4 308330
Website	www.weaverpresszimbabwe.com
Contact	Njabulo Mbono

Weaver Press is a small publishing house committed to the production and distribution of the best of Zimbabwe's creative writing and scholarly research. It was established in 1998, since when it has developed a solid reputation for excellent editorial and production standards. As well as publishing contemporary fiction, we work with researchers and academic authors to produce books which reflect the developing tensions, challenges and prospects for Zimbabwean society; we also, on occasion, undertake freelance editing and typesetting.

Creative Writing Course
- Available online and face-to-face in Johannesburg and Cape Town
- Learn the skills needed to write a novel or a work of creative non-fiction
- Receive personal feedback on all writing assignments

Mentoring Programme
- Designed to help you start or finish your book
- Over a six month period you'll be mentored online, via Skype and/or in face-to-face sessions
- Suitable for writers who have completed a substantial writing course

www.allaboutwritingcourses.com

info@allaboutwritingcourses.com

Wits University Press

Address	5th Floor, University Corner, University of the Witwatersrand
	Cnr Jan Smuts Avenue and Jorissen Street
	Braamfontein, Johannesburg, South Africa
Post	Private Bag 3, PO Wits, 2050
Email	info.witspress@wits.ac.za
Phone	+ 27 11 717 8700/8701
Website	www.witspress.co.za
Contact	Veronica Klipp

WITS UNIVERSITY PRESS

Wits University Press is scholarly publisher strategically placed at the crossroads of African and global knowledge production and dissemination. We are committed to publishing well-researched, innovative books for both academic and general readers. Our areas of focus include art and heritage, popular science, history and politics, biography, literary studies, women's writing and select textbooks. If you'd like to publish with Wits University Press, please consult our submission guidelines on our website – www.witspress.co.za. Our books are distributed by Blue Weaver Marketing & Distribution (021 701 4477), orders@blueweaver.co.za.

Wordweaver Publishing House

Address   Gruner Krantz Complex, Macadam Street (Opposite Obeco)

Southern Industrial area, Windhoek

Post   P O Box 5026, Ausspannplatz, Windhoek

Website   www.wordweavernam.com

Unlike most existing publishing houses in Namibia who focus only on educational material, Wordweaver publishes a wide range of genres. Wordweaver was established as a response to the incredible talent of Namibian writers and the difficulties they faced in getting published. Wordweaver believes that there is a world-wide audience for their stories. Published books range from fiction, children's stories to adult and include all genres. Though currently not interested in historical titles, they will definitely publish some coffee table non-fiction work as well.

Classifieds

Liz Sparg

Do you need a writer, editor, proofreader or project manager? Liz Sparg (MA Linguistics) has a solid reputation, with 22 years in the business and a variety of established clients. View her profile on LinkedIn and contact Liz: lizjuliesparg@gmail.com, +27 82 730 5293

Andy Thesen, Desktop Publishing Services

Wide experience in many roles in the publishing industry. Offering support to self-publishers.

- Editorial: Copy-editing and proofreading
- Productions: Book design, typesetting and layout
- Print: Work with printers to manage quotes and printing
- Ebooks: Convert ebooks for digital platforms and POD.

Contact me to chat or for a quote: athesen@global.co.za or +27 82 725 8801.

Articles

African Books Collective: 25 years of the best in African publishing

JUSTIN COX

Indigenous publishing is integral to national identity and development: cultural, social, and economic. Such publishing reflects a people's history and experience, belief systems, and their concomitant expressions through language, writing, and art. In turn, a people's interaction with other cultures is informed by their published work. Publishing preserves, enhances, and develops a society's culture and its interaction with others. In Africa, indigenous publishers continue to seek autonomy to pursue these aims: free from the constraints of the colonial past, the strictures of economic structural adjustment policies, the continuing dominance of multinational publishers (particularly in textbooks), regressive language policies, and lack of recognition by African governments of the economic and cultural importance of publishing.

– Bgoya, Walter & Jay, Mary "Publishing in Africa from Independence to the Present Day" in Research in African Literatures, Vol. 44, No. 2, Summer 2013, p. 1

It is in this context that African Books Collective (ABC) was founded in 1989 by a group of African publishers to supply libraries and other book buyers worldwide with African published books, and to assert Africa's own voice in the international marketplace on equal terms. ABC was established as a non-profit,  covering its overheads only, and remitting sales income to African publishers. On the one hand, ABC addresses the hurdles for Northern libraries in acquiring books from Africa; and on the other, strengthens African publishers by providing international exposure and valuable sales income. By the 1990s, the acute problems in African publishing had seen failures of many state and independent publishing houses, and international aid agencies and foundations provided support funding to a number of African book initiatives. Of those, ABC has uniquely remained, becoming self-sufficient from 2007 by capitalising on new digital initiatives, such as print-on-demand, ebooks, and digital marketing. ABC has been a key player in the digitisation of African cultural output since remodelling in 2007. Sales are on a slow but steady rise as are the number of new titles being received from Africa. Despite the doom and gloom statistics promoted by many international organisations, new African publishers continue to burgeon with no shortage of committed individuals with enough belief in the power of book publishing to want to operate in challenging market conditions. ABC publishers include university presses, research institutes, commercial presses – large and small, NGOs and writers' organisations. In 2016 ABC seeks to be the primary distribution choice for independent African publishers; to provide the most comprehensive selection of relevant material to customers worldwide in the form they require; to achieve ABC's cultural aims whilst operating in a wholly commercial space; and to grow the market for African books worldwide. In late 2015 the ABC online store was relaunched with a mobile friendly design and updated subject categories which showcase the diversity within African independent publishing. A second website will be launched in 2016 to compliment the online store: readafricanbooks.com will be focused on the wide promotion of African published books. Selected scholarship and writing will be available free, book reviews will be posted and specialist contributors will tell us their picks. The site will also include opinion about book issues in Africa from some of Africa's leading publishers and also others involved in the book trade. ABC hopes to continue some of the work done by APNET and the much loved Indabas at the Zimbabwe Book Fair some years ago: bringing publishers together, exchanging ideas, exploring new methods of cooperation and providing an outlet for the views of an industry with much change ahead.

One major area in which the collective would like to bring publishers together is the issue of book donations. Currently African-published books form little part of many African library collections Consequently African publishers cannot rely on library sales to improve the viability of their publishing projects. In response to the so-called "book famine" in Africa, both British and American organisations and individuals have responded with good intentions to send book donations to African libraries, schools and communities. These unrequested books are "free" to the libraries but the donation organisations must pay for shipping containers to Africa. That is a direct cost. To be seeking to assist libraries in a culturally sensitive way, rather than offloading unwanted or unsold books from the North, why should that cost not be diverted to a budget for libraries to select titles from within Africa? So many donation schemes talk about a million books donated here, ten-thousand there but very few discuss the sorts of books being received in Africa or how such quantities affect the wider book chain in African countries. Many bypass African publishers completely and promote the idea that no publishers exist in Africa, some who do include African published books pay so little for them it is debatable whether this strengthens or actually weakens African publishing. Some years ago donors collaborated with publishers to come up with sustainable solutions to the unique challenges within each country, it seems those days are not so common anymore, therefore it is the intention of readafricanbooks.com to let the world know that African publishers are still interested, committed, and able to contribute solutions to those challenges.

Because we have sooo many stories to tell you

NYANA KAKOMA

When I started the blog, Sooo Many Stories, I had no big plans for the blog but my desire to showcase Ugandan literature always left me restless. I had been in a couple of spaces with non Ugandan writers and readers and I was shocked when I often found that they could not name any Ugandan writers or recall Ugandan stories (stories

about Uganda or written by Ugandan writers). But what was even more shocking was that even the most avid of Ugandan readers were not reading any literature by Ugandans. For someone that was just starting to convince myself that writing was not the wrong dream for me, the thought of never being read was very scary. Why bother if I was never going to be read?

And so Sooo Many Stories was born. To shine a light on Ugandan stories from our legends and myths to stories that were orally passed on from generation to generation as a record of our past and as a way of teaching lessons to our fictional stories.

One of my biggest surprises was how writers, most of them upcoming, were very willing to trust me with their work and their courage to share their work and allow strangers into their worlds. It is also always very encouraging to meet readers asking for more, and commenting on the works of different writers.

Important was also the need to write about the different opportunities that are there in Uganda and internationally for all sorts of writers. To open up the space beyond their little cocoons to competitions, residencies and other opportunities that would take writing and storytelling to the next level.

As the person running the blog, I found myself pushing myself, wanting to learn more; be a better editor and find out as much as I could about publishing. It was through this that I was able to apply for an editorial workshop in Kampala that further opened the world of editing and publishing to me. To learn that it was beyond making sure that the right sentences followed each other but that the voice of the writer was clear and their vision well executed was something that made me attach more importance to what I was doing with writers. But even then, the blog was still just that, a blog.

Until my internship with Modjaji in February/March 2015 courtesy of African Writers Trust, my vision was just limited to the blog. I knew of the publishing void in Uganda and the lack of structures to encourage a better reading culture but I had never been in a place that would make me so angry about our lack and at the same time stir up a desire to do more. But the more I learnt about different publishing models, the more I wanted for us as writers and I started to believe that we could do a lot better.

And now, what started as a blog is a publishing house. With our first collection of poetry underway, we hope to be the answer to the lack of good fiction and nonfiction for adults and young adults. I wait for the day in 2016 when we shall launch our first book with the joyful anticipation of one waiting for the birth of their child.

I hope our stories get to be told. I hope our children get to read characters that they can relate with. I hope we get to win international awards and get international recognition and I hope that dreaming of being a writer won't seem like dreaming the wrong dream. That's what Sooo Many Stories is about.

The International Declaration of Independent Publishers 2014

INTERNATIONAL ALLIANCE OF INDEPENDENT PUBLISHERS

The International Assembly of independent publishers 2012-2014 was held over two years, **through seven preparatory and thematic workshops** held in Guadalajara (Mexico), Paris (France), Bologna (Italy), Ouagadougou (Burkina Faso), Frankfurt (Germany) and Abu Dhabi (United Arab Emirates) and **a closing meeting held under the patronage of UNESCO,** in Cape Town (South Africa) at the Centre for the Book, from 18 to 21 September 2014.

Preparatory workshops, completed through working groups, focused on themes selected and prioritised by publishers (**digital publishing, public book policies, independent publishing houses' economic models, youth literature, national and local languages publishing, solidarity publishing partnerships and 'Fair Trade Book', book donations**). From these workshops and on-line exchanges 80 recommendations were developed, aimed at public authorities, international organisations and book professionals, discussed, and validated by publishers who convened in Cape Town in September 2014. The objectives of these 80 proposals (see bit.ly/IAIP80) are **to support and promote bibliodiversity at both national and international levels.**

Delegates to the IAIP conference in September 2014

This whole process led to the drafting of the 2014 International Declaration of independent publishers. On 20 September 2014, **60 independent publishers from 38 countries present in Cape Town collectively drafted, in three languages, their policy statement.** For more than four hours of interlinguistic and intercultural exchanges, joint reflection, mutual respect and questioning, publishers drafted this statement. The 2014 Declaration was also validated on-line by absent publishers and is currently being translated into several languages (French, English, Spanish, Portuguese, Arabic, Farsi, Italian, etc.). To date, **400 publishers from 45 countries signed the International Declaration of independent publishers,** that you can widely distribute to promote and strengthen bibliodiversity with us.

International Declaration of Independent Publishers 2014, to promote and strengthen bibliodiversity together

Preamble

The book is essential for building and spreading knowledge, in the shaping of a human being and development of a critical mind. It is not simply a commodity. As a cultural asset, it forms part of a certain kind of economy which should not be subject to market forces exclusively. Its design, production and marketing, whether in print or digital format, should enable a book to last, since it is intended as much for future generations as for those in the present.

The independent publisher has total freedom in the design of editorial policy, which s/he carries out autonomously. Her/his approach is not solely commercial. Together with the other actors in the book chain, s/he is the guarantor of creativity, of ensuring that histories of oppression and suppression are kept alive, of the democratisation of books as well as of diverse and critical publishing. S/he is also the crafter of essential bibliodiversity. S/he prioritizes quality and longevity over mass production and speed.

Independent publishers find themselves increasingly weakened by the consequences of neo-liberal policies and the resulting corporatization of the publishing industry. Over the past few years, the rise of the large digital players has further intensified this situation: they consider cultural content to be simple instruments which serve their financial interests.

Political developments have an impact on the fate of cultural actors. In certain countries, democratic changes have opened up platforms for freedom and allowed a new generation of independent publishers to emerge. In other countries, on the other hand, conflicts severely affect publishing activity and the freedom to express a variety of opinions.

Within this context, independent publishing nevertheless manages to renew itself and to make diverse voices heard. Independent publishing is still thriving not only out of necessity but also because publishers have been able to mobilise themselves so as to be heard and to join forces. Today, more than ever, solidarity is vital.

Declaration

We, 400 publishers from 45 countries, meeting in the framework of the International Alliance of Independent Publishers at our Third Assembly, held in Cape Town (South Africa) in September 2014, reaffirm **our will to act together to defend and promote bibliodiversity.**

In 2005, the adoption by UNESCO of the *Convention on the Protection and Promotion of the Diversity of Cultural Expressions*, followed by its ratification by numerous States, represented an important step in recognising the specificity of cultural content and the role of the independent publisher. In order for it to be heeded, however, this Convention must be translated into pro-active public policies.

In countries where **national book policies** are weak or non-existent, we appeal to governments to establish without delay policies which foster cultural development and the democratisation of books and reading. All the actors in the book chain need to be very closely involved in drawing up and applying such policies. They must reinforce the book industry in each country and help support local production, distribution, and access by all to books; in particular by establishing adequate regulatory and fiscal measures, and by providing more space for reading, especially public libraries. Such policies should encompass printed books as much as digital and should promote their complementarity.

It is also crucial, in the context of globalisation, that national policies are carried over into **regional and international policies.** Such policies must allow books to circulate in an equitable manner and regulate the book market so that it is protected from the predatory acts of the large international e-tail and retail groups.

It is essential that fair laws regarding **copyright** be drawn up and applied, laws which allow for authors' rights be protected while guaranteeing access to knowledge.

We must be doubly vigilant and also doubly inventive if we are to thwart **any form of suppression of the word.** The struggle against all forms of **censorship** (State, administrative, religious, economic and even self-censorship) remains a priority.

Thought is not controlled by censorship alone. In an environment of excessive information, media concentration and the standardisation of content, it is essential to be careful that freedom of expression does not only serve the voice of the dominant groups or powers. **We, the independent publishers, defend Fair Speech** in order to make a multiplicity of voices heard, which in itself secures bibliodiversity.

The digital players in a hegemonic position, such as Amazon, Google or Apple, should not be above the laws and fiscal regulations in force in any country. We call on public authorities and on international bodies to pass laws which encourage bibliodiversity, so that publishers and bookshops may continue to play their indispensable role as cultural actors and intermediaries.

The distribution of books should not be uni-directional, reproducing situations of dominance and preventing the development of local markets and national industries. We call for equitable exchanges between large book-exporting countries and those countries that import books.

Regarding **textbooks**, the State and the large international publishing groups tend to dominate markets in the countries of the Global South, despite the advocacy of professional collectives and the existence of policy measures. It is urgent that local independent publishers be allowed to take over the production of textbooks, which is essential for strengthening the local book economy and developing other less lucrative and more risky publishing sectors. In particular, it is vital for young readers' development that they should be able to relate to the material given to them.

Donations of printed books, as well as digital devices (e-readers, tablets...) and digital content, even when motivated by philanthropic principles, contribute to a certain cultural hegemony. The warnings given by Southern professionals and their proposals for other types of book donation have contributed to a change in such practices. It is important that this system continues to be questioned across the world to provide a sustainable response to readers' needs and expectations.

Professional solidarity among independent publishers is a force that counters such predatory structures. We need to develop our own tools and encourage the transfer of skills as well as the sharing of know-how and resources.

Exchange of literature and ideas between countries **through translations** is an important promoter of mutual knowledge and is essential for the development of a critical, democratic approach. Funds to support translation must be established and strengthened. In order to encourage intercultural dialogue and preserve bibliodiversity, reciprocal translations should be supported.

Co-publishing and the principle of the 'fair trade book' facilitate the exchange of content and ideas. They allow publishing costs and activities to be shared and books to be offered to the broadest public at a fair price. We are convinced that these practices need to be extended, especially through recourse to funds offering assistance for co-publishing.

Despite its essential role in sustainable education and social development, publishing in **local and national languages** continues to be marginalised. We need to promote the transmission of knowledge and emancipation, and ensure that each community has access to reading material in its own language.

We call on independent publishers everywhere in the world to come together, alongside the authors, independent bookstores, librarians and other actors in the book chain, and to form associations and collectives allowing bibliodiversity to thrive and become stronger.

Finally, **it is our responsibility, as independent publishers,** to practise the principles we have set out and to defend a publishing model which respects human rights and the environment. We also have a responsibility to readers and to people with little access to books, since a democratic approach depends on the acquisition of knowledge by each one of us. Together we must count on our ability to act and to redouble our creativity.

My year of South African fiction

PENNY DE VRIES

I have been hungrily devouring SA Fiction for many years; in my twenties it was André Brink, in my thirties it was JM Coetzee, in my forties it was Zakes Mda and Marlene van Niekerk. Quality writing but slim pickings in terms of variety.

In September 2014, a thread in The Good Book Appreciation Society Facebook Group got me thinking. The discussion was about how so much fiction by SA writers is being published these days; one person commented that you could read SA Fiction for a whole year and not run out. I thought, imagine doing that, only reading SA Fiction for a whole year; it could be an interesting challenge. It seemed akin to birding (my other passion) as I keep year lists of all the birds I see in a year in the Southern African region. I have always kept a list of books I read every year so why not do a Book Big Year? Focus my reading on a geographical region.

On the spur of that moment I decided that in 2015 I would devote myself to reading only SA Fiction. I also thought it would be more meaningful if I wrote a review on each book and published it in a blog. I even hoped this might help spread the word about SA Fiction in a small way. I was dying for January 1 2015 to arrive so I could begin. I made a list of possible books and in December I went shopping. The tantalising pile sat on my coffee table for a few weeks.

Within a few months I realised that my reading experience had been greatly enhanced. Although I am not an indiscriminate reader, previously I had often found myself reading books that I had been urged to read and then not enjoying them that much. For 2015, I selected the books that I wanted to read. I was particularly interested in reading more black writers; I had already read and enjoyed all three of Thando Mqolozana's books as well as most of Zakes Mda's books. I also wanted to find novels set in different parts of South Africa. I had complained that so many novels are set in Cape Town; this precipitated a deluge of suggestions of novels set elsewhere. I read books set in the Natal Midlands, Durban, Johannesburg, North-West Province, Limpopo, Zimbabwe, Mozambique, London, Mossel Bay, Northern Cape and Pietermaritzburg.

The most fascinating thing that emerged was the recurring themes that kept cropping up. Perhaps I should have predicted what they would be but I had not really thought about it in advance. Rape is a highly prevalent topic; usually by men preying on vulnerable young girls, whether a pastor in a township, a farmer in the Midlands or a school principal but also boys being raped by a family friend or relative. That so many writers independently write about rape speaks for itself. Stemming from this is the theme of mixed parentage; so many secrets kept because for so many years, sex across the colour line was illegal, thus the children often had their true parentage kept from them.

Other common themes are disaffected youth, drugs, gangs, HIV, the effects on families and communities of apartheid and continuing oppression by whites, clashes within families and communities between traditional and modern beliefs, corruption and abuse of power.

It is has also been a treat to read so many novels in which the language used is remarkable. I have, in the main, enjoyed the writing,

plotting, characterisation and dialogue. Out of the 52 books I read in 2015, there are only 2 or 3 that I did not like.

Writing about the books meant I read less than I usually would. I skim read each book a second time to ensure my reviews were accurate. This turned out to be one of the most rewarding things because there are often things that one misses on the first reading. Part of the fun is checking the stats on my blog. This registers number of visitors, number of views and country from where the visitor is accessing the blog. After South African viewers, America and Canada are the next highest. It even received visitors from Oman, Latvia, Mali and Croatia. Who would have thought there would be people there interested in SA Fiction?

My reading experience has been richer this year than ever before. I know I will not return to my previous way of reading. Next year I am going to focus on reading more novels from the rest of Africa but not to the exclusion of all else.

Short Story Day Africa: Punching above our weight

RACHEL ZADOK

Over the past decade, the publishing industry has become risk-averse. The words 'genre-defying' and 'original' make agents and editors break out in a cold sweat – or so we're told. The industry is constantly described as conservative. Manuscripts are rejected for being too cerebral, unsellable in a market that wants only apple pie. Alternative publishing models have developed for writers looking for new routes to readers. However, the indie publishers behind this groundswell are often (unfairly) perceived as exploitative; and the work they produce is dismissed as subpar.

It is in this climate that Short Story Day Africa was formed. In the five years since inception, the SSDA team has developed a survival ethos: to subvert and reclaim. Reclaim the place of the short story. Reclaim a space for non-conformist writing. Subvert ideas about what it means to be a writer in Africa. Subvert ideas about what makes a story African.

What began as a simple idea to celebrate short stories on the shortest day of the year swiftly transformed into a platform providing support to African writers, both emerging and established, and a hub of information for readers.

The Short Story Day Africa Prize is now in its fourth year, and has launched or boosted the careers of dozens of writers from all over the continent and diaspora. Our 2013 anthology, *Feast, Famine & Potluck*, resulted in two Caine Prize-nominated short stories, including the winning story, 'My Father's Head' by Okwiri Oduor. The 2014 anthology, *Terra Incognita*, which has speculative fiction as its focus, also featured Caine-nominated writers such as Diane Awerbuck among emerging and established stars. *Terra Incognita* was widely acclaimed, and received a glowing review in the *L.A. Review of Books*, amongst others.

The year-on-year growth in entries to the annual Short Story Day Africa Prize is indicative of the project's success. In 2013, we received 62 entries for *Feast, Famine & Potluck*. By the following year, that number had grown to 106. In 2015, we received a staggering 456 entries for our third collection, *Water*. These numbers confirm the need for publishing platforms and hubs to nurture writing talent beyond university creative writing degrees and commercially oriented writing courses. They also testify to the ferment of creative energy emerging from Anglophone Africa and the diaspora – a wellspring often given short shrift in the pinched climate of international publishing.

More than a creative writing competition, the prize serves as a workshop in short story writing. Through the annual prize, we identify up to twenty-one promising writers from the continent and, over a period of three/four months, work to develop their stories with two professional editors. The editors work closely with the writers to hone voice and technique, while imparting years of industry wisdom and teaching the all-important craft of story-telling. The editing process becomes a master-class in story-telling, a privilege usually reserved for those with the resources to participate in university creative writing programmes. The process is transformative, both for stories and writers.

We have identified a further need to develop editors as well as writers. To this end, we have created a paid editing mentorship for young editors wishing to establish a career in the field. The 2016 anthology will be Short Story Day Africa's first anthology that will work to develop the skills of both writers and editors on the continent.

Short Story Day Africa's online sites supply a constant stream of writing tips, submission and writing residencies opportunities, festival news, author interviews and story links. In addition, a bi-monthly event called #WriterPrompt is held on Facebook. As the project's popularity has risen, so has the quality of anthology submissions. This has meant that writers new to the industry stand little chance of publication unless they get opportunities to up their game, show their skills and attract peer interaction. SSDA provides a prompt, and writers post flash fiction on the event page inspired by the prompt. They are then encouraged provide constructive feedback on fellow participants' stories. One story from each event is featured on our website, along with a short interview with the author.

In the digital age, literary projects are a dime a dozen. Many collapse under the weight of their own ambition as quickly as they spring up. What makes SSDA different is not only the collaborative nature of the project and the team's willingness to evolve, but an appreciation of the literary aesthetic. While we reclaim a space for non-conformist African writing, we acknowledge that the world is now a global village. The work we produce stands alongside the best work produced anywhere, at any time in history, and we believe, will stand in the future. Given the modest beginnings of this project, we're amazed, grateful and a bit unnerved by the speed at which SSDA has grown, and the extent of its reach. But we're blown away by the talent, ideas and tenacity it has revealed to us, and proud to play a small part in sharing this with a wider audience. Out of Africa, something always new: indeed.

Book Dash, growing new readers in South Africa

ARTHUR ATTWELL

I like to imagine that I'm a pharmaceutical rep, and I'm selling a drug that's been proven to dramatically enhance brain development in young children. It's been proven to be safe, and it's easy and quick to administer – in fact, children love it so much they ask for it.

Till now, only wealthy families have been able to afford the drug: till now, it cost about R6 per day, which is over R10000 by the age of five. But – now! – we've found a way to reduce that cost tenfold: to less than 56 cents a day (that's USD0.05). And we reckon it's time that, as a country, we started giving it to poor families to give their kids a boost.

That drug, of course, is a book. And we've found a way that just 56 cents a day can buy a child a hundred books by the age of five.[1]

That's also our vision at non-profit organisation Book Dash – what we want for the world: *every child should own a hundred books by the age of five.*

Our books are produced by teams of professional writers, illustrators and designers, volunteering their time to create new children's books that anyone, anywhere, is free to download and adapt, translate, print, republish, sell or give away.

When you print 5000 copies or more of a book, it costs less than R10 a book. At that price, a child can have a hundred books in five years for 56 cents day.

I'll explain how we're making that possible, and why it's important and special.

But, first, why do I think it's necessary to create and give away free, paper books? Surely the publishing industry is growing the market? Surely ebook technology is solving our problems?

I'm a book publisher, and I worked in big educational publishing companies for many years. And I happen to have an especially strong love–hate relationship with technology. I'm a keen technologist, I live and breathe technology, and yet I think technology is our age's greatest distraction to real progress, and our biggest money waster.

Back in 2006 I left my corporate publishing job, sold my little red sports car, and struck out with some friends to start Electric Book Works, a small agency where I wanted to reimagine publishing for emerging markets, using technology sensibly and humbly.

South Africa is so very different from the places we inherited our publishing industry from; the UK and the US in particular. We inherited their royalty schemes and bookshop relationships and price points and technologies and job descriptions. But our languages, our histories, our physical spaces, our ambitions and our daily lives are different.

So the book publishing industry, as it stands, doesn't really work here. And by 'really work' I mean it has not and cannot make books a part of everyone's lives.

Over the years I've tried dozens of experiments to tackle this problem: I've published ebooks with musical soundtracks (they didn't catch on), a self-publishing service, a youth magazine. My biggest recent project was Paperight, where we were funded by the Shuttleworth Foundation to turn copy shops into print-on-demand bookstores. And our longest-running project is Bettercare, which creates learning programmes for nurses that anyone can use online for free.

The point is to keep trying something else, anything that isn't the usual way of doing things, because the usual way has left our country with very few, very expensive books.

After all my experimenting, I've come to believe that there are no 'market solutions' to growing a book-loving nation. For most South Africans, books are a luxury they can't afford, not when food and clothing is already hard to come by.

Recent research from UCT's Unilever Institute showed that most families in South Africa live on less than R6000 a month. They regularly turn off the fridge before the end of the month – they're out of electricity, and there's no food in it anyway. Many of them skip meals towards the end of the month. It's mad to think they'll ever be able to buy books, at any price.

The only way to grow readers is the hard way: we simply must give away vast numbers of free books to young children.

And this isn't some idealistic third-world charity idea. In the UK, for eight years already, every school-going child has been given free books on World Book Day. Why do our children deserve any less?

I'm not the only one who wants to give away free books: many great organisations are trying to do the same. The Shine Centre is a shining example. But they have to buy expensive books from publishers to do it, and there are very, very few books available that are:

- new, high-quality stories created here
- with scenes and characters our children recognise
- in languages they speak
- beautiful enough to love for a lifetime.

Why are books like this so rare and expensive? Well, traditional publishing is an expensive process.

When you pay, say, R100 for a book in a bookstore, you're paying for writing, development, editing, design, proofreading, the to-and-fro of disks and paper, project management, marketing, sales, printing, ebook conversion, shipping, warehousing, wastage, the retailer's cut, returns of unsold books, the publisher's profit, and VAT. And in between each of those pieces there is a lot of expensive time wasting.

This process is expensive, requires rare professional skills, and takes a long time. The average book-production process, after writing is complete, is about six months.

It's also hugely competitive, especially in children's books. This all makes publishing very risky. It's almost impossible to make back your investment as a South African children's book publisher, especially when you're up against imported books that were created in London or New York and shipped all over the world in massive quantities.

Most children's books published in South Africa are effectively cross-subsidised by textbook sales to government schools.

This is why there are so few South African children's books. And why so few are in African languages. In 2013, the latest year we have stats for, of R312 million in local trade publishing revenue, only R1.7 million, or 0.5%, came from books in our nine official African languages.

But here's an interesting thing about the cost of book publishing: *book publishing is 90% air and wages.*

What I mean is that if you were to squeeze it like a sponge, removing all the air – time and delay – and the wages, you could still make beautiful books, but for a fraction of the cost, in a fraction of the time. The trick is knowing how and what to squeeze.

So to start Book Dash we asked professional writers, illustrators, designers and editors to volunteer their time to create new, high-quality, African children's books.

First, we put them in teams. Each team has a writer, an illustrator, and a designer, and twelve hours to create one book. Usually the writers have developed the idea for their story in advance, and the illustrators have thrown together some concept sketches. Expert editors then work with each team to help refine their story. We also bring in art directors and tech support, in a great venue, with great food and lots of coffee.

The room buzzes with creative energy and inspiration. We call it the Comrades Marathon of creativity: not just for the long, hard day, but for the incredible solidarity it produces.

Before our first Book Dash, I was secretly worried about the quality of the books we'd get. But what we found was astonishing: the books are just so good, and so beautiful. Committed volunteers really bring their best, because they know this is a rare chance to do something special.

Also, real-time teamwork knits the writing, illustration and design together powerfully – something that's almost impossible in lengthy, traditional publishing workflows. One of our volunteer editors, who works by day for big publishing companies, said that this is how all children's books should be created: with the creators sitting around a table together thrashing out every spread.

Most importantly, all our work is our gift to the world: everything is open-licensed on the day so that anyone afterwards can download, translate, print, and distribute it.

Already our books are being reused in print and digital forms around South Africa and beyond. Nal'ibali, the national reading campaign, has reused and translated our books in their newspaper story supplements, and they contribute those translations back to us. The African Storybook Project (who've sponsored two Book Dashes before) has republished and translated them for use online in several African countries. And we're working with FunDza and Worldreader to put them on mobile phones here and around the world.

We've used crowdfunding, partnerships and corporate sponsorship to print and give away over seventeen thousand books in our first eighteen months, which is a small but promising start. They've gone to children and libraries in literacy programs, ECD projects, schools and daycare centres. We've just raised enough to print another fifty thousand.

When we give books away, we go and meet some of the children and give them books in person. And there's nothing more wonderful for me, as a book publisher, than to give a book to a three-year-old and see them dash to a corner, open it up and start reading.

After all my experimenting, that's the result I've been looking for. And I look forward to the day those children grow up and take our publishing industry to places we can only dream of.

1. 100 books over 5 years is 20 books per year, or 1.67 books per month. At R10 a book that's R16.70 per month, or 56c per day.